God Is With Me
I Am Not Afraid

A WEEKLY INFUSION OF POWER

By

L. O. Ovbije

ISBN: 978-1-944411-02-2

Copyright © 2017 by Rev. L O. Ovbije
Ovbije World Outreach Ministries, Inc.
P.O. Box 966
Clarkston, GA 30021-0966
U. S. A.
Website: owom.org
Email: theword@owom.org

Published by SOIL Foundation, Inc.
P.O. Box 966
Clarkston, GA 30021-0966
U. S. A.

All scriptures are from King James Version (KJV)
Printed in the United States of America.
All rights reserved under International Copyright Law. Contents and/ or cover may not be reproduced in whole or in part in any form, electronic or mechanical, including photocopying, recording, or by any information storage and retrieval system, without the express written consent of the Publisher.

DEDICATION

This book is dedicated to my precious, wonderful and lovely parents Chief J. E. Ovbije & Mrs. Margaret Orhe Edokpaghare Ovbije: the greatest parents God ever created on earth. I am forever grateful to God for my parents and I am exceedingly thankful to God for my parents and abundant of thanks to my wonderful and lovely parents. Father I thank you for the safety and security you instill in me from infanthood through my parents. Their present in my life and at home gave me great safety and security from childhood. I thank God for my parent's unconditional love for me. Where there is love there is safety, security, no fear and self-value. God loves me, God said to me in the Bible "He is Love" and he said also "He will never leave me nor forsake me". Just as I trust my parents, I trust God. My parents never lied to me, God will never lie.

ACKNOWLEDGMENTS

To my wonderful parents Chief J. E. Ovbije & Mrs. Margaret O. Ovbije, and to my siblings. My father was a man that lived a life that left an excellent and lasting impression on me. Our family knew the meaning of a loving, secure and rich home because of my father's presence. I thank God for the private elementary school at Sapele: Children Nursery School, where I attended. It was there that I encounter God for the first time in prayer in a very early age.

To my precious pastor and his lovely wife, both were strong examples of a man and a woman devoted to God. I was fortunate to have pastor & Mrs. Umukoro, both disciples me. I thank them both for their daily early morning prayer life. To the men of God who also impacted my prayer life, W. F. Kumuyi and Benjamin Udi.

Finally to my sweet, precious, wonderful wife Theresa Spearman Ovbije, a woman of God, whom I simply call "sweetie"

WEEK ONE

Fear thou not; for I am with thee…
Isaiah 41:10

God Is With Me

After these things the word of the LORD came unto Abram in a vision, saying, Fear not, Abram: I am thy shield, and thy exceeding great reward.
Genesis 15:1

Boldly Say: Father, I thank you that you are my shield and my exceeding great reward. I thank you Father that you command me not to fear, because you did not give me the spirit of fear, but you have given me the spirit of power, the spirit of love, and the spirit of a sound mind. Therefore, I do boldly confess that I do not have the spirit of fear, but I do possess the spirit of power, I do possess the spirit of love, and I do possess the spirit of a sound mind. Father, I thank you that you do speak to me in my dreams. I thank you that in my dreams you do show me things to come and you do instruct me how to pray about things you show me.

2 TIMOTHY 1:7

WEEK TWO

Fear thou not; for I am with thee...
Isaiah 41:10

God Is With Me

And God heard the voice of the lad; and the angel of God called to Hagar out of heaven, and said unto her, What aileth thee, Hagar? fear not; for God hath heard the voice of the lad where he is. ***Genesis 21:17***

Boldly Say: **Father I thank you that I am not alone for you are always with me. Father I thank you that when no one understand me, when all abandon me, you are still with me. I am never alone and I will never be alone**

because you are always with me. God is with me now, and he is with me forever, regardless how I feel, I refuse to fear. I am not afraid.

2 TIMOTHY 1:7

WEEK THREE

**Fear thou not; for I am with thee…
Isaiah 41:10**

God Is With Me

*And the L*ORD *appeared unto him the same night, and said, I am the God of Abraham thy father: fear not, for I am with thee, and will bless thee, and multiply thy seed for my servant Abraham's sake.*
Genesis 26:24

<u>*Boldly Say:*</u> **Father I thank you for the blood of Jesus Christ covenant I do have with you. Father, I thank you that because I accepted the sacrifice of the blood of Jesus Christ for my sin, I am redeemed, I am born again**

and I am your child. Therefore, I will not fear because the blood of Jesus Christ is applied to my life. Father I thank you for you are blessing me daily and multiplying my seed because of Jesus Christ. Father I thank you that the blood of Jesus Christ speaks of better things about me.

2 TIMOTHY 1:7

WEEK FOUR

Fear thou not; for I am with thee…
Isaiah 41:10

God Is With Me

And Moses said unto the people, Fear ye not, stand still, and see the salvation of the LORD, which he will shew to you to day: for the Egyptians whom ye have seen to day, ye shall see them again no more for ever.
Exodus 14:13

Boldly Say: **Father I thank you that whenever I face opposing circumstance, I will look to you to tell me what to do and act on your word, I will not fear the circumstance, I will apply your** written word, yes, I will stand against the opposition by doing your word regardless of my feelings. Yes, I will see your salvation for me pertaining to that circumstance.

2 TIMOTHY 1:7

WEEK FIVE

Fear thou not; for I am with thee…
Isaiah 41:10

God Is With Me

Behold, the LORD thy God hath set the land before thee: go up and possess it, as the LORD God of thy fathers hath said unto thee; fear not, neither be discouraged.
Deuteronomy 1:21

Boldly Say: Father I thank you for the life of Jesus Christ here on earth, I thank you for the example Jesus Christ left for me to follow daily, yes I can look to Jesus Christ daily, He alone paid the vicarious price for my sin, for he alone is the author and finisher of my faith, therefore, I am not afraid. Yes, I do go forth to possess my inheritance in Christ, fear cannot and will not stop me from my possession. All Jesus Christ paid for is mine.

2 TIMOTHY 1:7

WEEK SIX

Fear thou not; for I am with thee…
Isaiah 41:10

God Is With Me

Ye shall not fear them: for the LORD your God he shall fight for you.
Deuteronomy 3:22

<u>**Boldly Say:**</u> Father I thank you that you are always with me, therefore, I will not fear, I thank you that I am not afraid of fear. I thank you that I am not afraid of any circumstance, condition, situation, people, person, institution, groups and the devil, because you, my heavenly Father is with me. God Almighty does

fight for me always, and he does fight for me now. I am now living fearlessly and in the peace of Christ Jesus which passes all understanding.

2 TIMOTHY 1:7

WEEK SEVEN

Fear thou not; for I am with thee…
Isaiah 41:10

God Is With Me

And shall say unto them, Hear, O Israel, ye approach this day unto battle against your enemies: let not your hearts faint, fear not, and do not tremble, neither be ye terrified because of them;
Deuteronomy 20:3

Boldly Say: **Father I thank you that whatever situation, circumstance and condition I face today I will not let my heart be trouble or faint, I will not fear, I will not fear anyone face, for God is with me and I am not**

alone. I am not afraid of any kind of enemies. For my battle is God's battle, I do cast all my cares upon God for he cares for me greatly and I do rest in God.

2 TIMOTHY 1:7

WEEK EIGHT

Fear thou not; for I am with thee…
Isaiah 41:10

God Is With Me

Be strong and of a good courage, fear not, nor be afraid of them: for the LORD thy God, he it is that doth go with thee; he will not fail thee, nor forsake thee.
Deuteronomy 31:6

<u>Boldly Say:</u> Father, I thank you that you are my Father, I thank you that you are mostly just, you will not tell me to do what you have not prepare me to do or you will not enable me to do, You said to me be strong and of a good courage, I say yes

LORD, I receive your word, therefore, I am strong and I am of a good courage. You said you are with me, yes LORD, I do believe you are with me, and because you are with me, you are going with me, therefore, we are going together and both of us are in this together, and both of us are unbeatable.

2 TIMOTHY 1:7

WEEK NINE

Fear thou not; for I am with thee…
Isaiah 41:10

God Is With Me

And the LORD, he it is that doth go before thee; he will be with thee, he will not fail thee, neither forsake thee: fear not, neither be dismayed.
Deuteronomy 31:8

Boldly Say: Father, I thank you for going before me, Father I am grateful that you are already in my future. Father, I thank you that I am not alone, and I will never be alone because you are always with me. Father, I thank you that you said you will never leave me nor forsake me, therefore, I have nothing to worry about, and moreover you commanded me not to fear, therefore, I refuse to fear. I am your obedient child; therefore, I say boldly I am not afraid.

2 TIMOTHY 7

WEEK TEN

Fear thou not; for I am with thee…
Isaiah 41:10

God Is With Me

*And the L**ORD** said unto Joshua, Be not afraid because of them: for to morrow about this time will I deliver them up all slain before Israel: thou shalt hough their horses, and burn their chariots with fire.*
Joshua 11:6

<u>*Boldly Say:*</u> **Father in Jesus name, I thank you that you will reveal to me those that are against me, yea, even those that say they are my friend but are jealous of me and plotting**

against me, all you will reveal to me. Father, I acknowledge that the battle is not mine but yours. Father, I thank you that you will tell me what to do and I will obey you. Father I thank you that I am not afraid of them and their attitude, Amen.

2 TIMOTHY 7

WEEK ELEVEN

Fear thou not; for I am with thee…
Isaiah 41:10

God Is With Me

And Elijah said unto her, Fear not; go and do as thou hast said: but make me thereof a little cake first, and bring it unto me, and after make for thee and for thy son.
1 Kings 17:13

Boldly Say: In Jesus name, I refuse to fear the economy climate around me. I am not afraid to obey God in regard to my finances, I am not afraid of the movement of the stock market, I am not afraid of the banks stocks, I am not afraid of the oil stocks, I am not afraid to give to the works of God Almighty, I am not afraid to help people financially, I am not afraid to save financially, I am not afraid because God has commanded me not to fear. I dare to take God at his word. God is my very own Father, and I am his very own child, and God does take care of all my need. I am debt free; I owe no finance to any man. I am a free child of God.

2 TIMOTHY 1:7

WEEK TWELVE

Fear thou not; for I am with thee…
Isaiah 41:10

God Is With Me

And he answered, Fear not: for they that be with us are more than they that be with them.
2 Kings 6:16

Boldly Say: Father I thank you that I am not alone, for you are always with me. Father I thank you that you said in your word in Isaiah 54:15 "Behold, they shall surely gather together, but not by me: whosoever shall gather together against thee shall fall for thy sake." I boldly declare that all that gather together against me shall fall for my sake. I do belong to God Almighty, I am God's child and I am God's righteousness in Christ Jesus. I refuse to fear. I boldly declare in Jesus name, I am not afraid, and what can man do unto me? Greater is God in me than the devil that is in the world.

2 TIMOTHY 1:7

WEEK THIRTEEN

Fear thou not; for I am with thee…
Isaiah 41:10

God Is With Me

And the covenant that I have made with you ye shall not forget; neither shall ye fear other gods.
2 Kings 17:38

Boldly Say: Father I thank you for the blood covenant you made with me, yes, and the covenant is in the blood of Jesus Christ. It is an everlasting covenant. That covenant declared boldly that you are the only True God. You are my very own Father and I am your very own child. You told me not to fear other gods. I am your obedient child therefore; I do not fear other gods. Father, I thank you that because I am redeemed by the precious blood of Jesus Christ and I am your child, no curse can manifest in or on me.

2 TIMOTHY 1:7

WEEK FOURTEEN

Fear thou not; for I am with thee…
Isaiah 41:10

God Is With Me

Ye shall not need to fight in this battle: set yourselves, stand ye still, and see the salvation of the LORD with you, O Judah and Jerusalem: fear not, nor be dismayed; to morrow go out against them: for the LORD will be with you.
2 Chronicles 20:17

<u>**Boldly Say:**</u> **Father I thank you that in every situation I face in life, I will seek your mind about the situation, and do what you will have me to do, instead of al-**

lowing fear. God did not give me the spirit of fear, but of power, and of love, and of a sound mind. No matter what I face, in Jesus name, I refuse to fear because God did not give me the spirit of fear. I boldly declare my battle is God's battle; I boldly cast all my cares upon God for he cares for me. Therefore, I boldly and firmly say I have no care.

2 TIMOTHY 1:7

WEEK FIFTEEN

**Fear thou not; for I am with thee…
Isaiah 41:10**

God Is With Me

Yea, though I walk through the valley of the shadow of death, I will fear no evil: for thou art with me; thy rod and thy staff they comfort me.
Psalm 23:4

<u>Boldly Say:</u> Father I thank you that though I walk through the valley of the shadow of death, I will fear no evil: for thou art with me; thy rod and thy staff they comfort me. Yes, I am never alone, for the Great God Almighty who created the heaven

and the earth, and all that is therein is with me. Therefore, I am not afraid, fear is foreign to me, for God did not give me the spirit of fear, I refuse and reject fear in any form, and I only have what God has given me.

2 TIMOTHY 1:7

WEEK SIXTEEN

Fear thou not; for I am with thee…
Isaiah 41:10

God Is With Me

The L<small>ORD</small> is my light and my salvation; whom shall I fear? the L<small>ORD</small> is the strength of my life; of whom shall I be afraid?
Psalm 27:1

<u>**Boldly Say:**</u> Father I thank you in Jesus name that you are my light and my salvation; whom shall I fear? The LORD God Almighty is the strength of my life; of whom shall I be afraid? Father I thank you because you are my very own Father, I am not afraid of anybody. Father I

thank you that I do not fear man, because you did not give me the spirit of fear, but you have given the spirit of power, and of love and of a sound mind. I boldly confess that I do possess the spirit of power, I do possess the spirit of love and I do possess the spirit of a sound mind.

2 TIMOTHY 1:7

WEEK SEVENTEEN

Fear thou not; for I am with thee…
Isaiah 41:10

God Is With Me

Though an host should encamp against me, my heart shall not fear: though war should rise against me, in this will I be confident.
Psalm 27:3

<u>Boldly Say:</u> **Father I thank you that though troubles, pains, problems, disappointments, all kinds of negative situations, conditions, circumstances and things may confront me or I may face, I forever settled it in my heart that I am not alone,**

God is my Father and he is always with me, therefore I am not afraid. Yes, I am not afraid of war in the spirit realm or in the natural realm; I do belong to God Almighty.

2 TIMOTHY 1:7

WEEK EIGHTEEN

Fear thou not; for I am with thee...
Isaiah 41:10

God Is With Me

Therefore will not we fear, though the earth be removed, and though the mountains be carried into the midst of the sea;
Psalm 46:2
<u>**Boldly Say:**</u> Father I thank you that your word is truth. I thank you that I do have a firm Foundation, and that Foundation is Jesus Christ. Therefore, I am not afraid of anything. Though the sea roared, though the mountains quark and produce great fire, though it thunder

aloud, though the sky pour down massive amount of rain water, and though the earth shake violently, I am still secure in Jesus Christ, and God is my present help in time of trouble, therefore, I am not afraid and I have no fear, for God is my very own Father and I am his very own child.

2 TIMOTHY 1:7

WEEK NINETEEN

Fear thou not; for I am with thee…
Isaiah 41:10

God Is With Me

In God I will praise his word, in God I have put my trust; I will not fear what flesh can do unto me.
Psalm 56:4
<u>***Boldly Say:***</u> **Father I praise you, I worship you, I adore you, I magnify the name of Jesus, for the name of Jesus is above every other name, at the name of Jesus every knee shall bow and every tongue shall confess that Jesus Christ is Lord, to the glory of God Almighty. Father I thank**

you that the name of Jesus is above fear, Father I thank you that I am save by Jesus name, I am baptized into the name of Jesus, Father you gave the name of Jesus to me to use in any circumstance, and Jesus name is above fear. Therefore, I fear no flesh or anyone or things.

2 TIMOTHY 1:7

WEEK TWENTY

Fear thou not; for I am with thee…
Isaiah 41:10

God Is With Me

The LORD is on my side; I will not fear: what can man do unto me?
Psalm 118:6

<u>*Boldly Say:*</u> Father I thank you that you are on my side, what can man do unto me? God is in me and God is with me. God will never leave me nor forsake me. I am God's beloveth, God made me his supreme creature. I am his favourite, because I am a doer of God's Word. I am God's ambassador on earth. The king-

dom of God is in me. I represent the kingdom of God on earth. There is nothing any man can do to me.

2 TIMOTHY 1:7

WEEK TWENTY-ONE

Fear thou not; for I am with thee…
Isaiah 41:10

God Is With Me

But whoso hearkeneth unto me shall dwell safely, and shall be quiet from fear of evil.
Proverbs 1:33

Boldly Say: Father I thank you that I am your child and I do obey you. I thank you that your word is a lamp unto my feet and a light unto my path. Father I thank you that your word have I hiding in my heart that I may not sin against thee. Father I thank you that your word is sweeter than honey to my taste.

O! God how wonderful is your word. Father I thank you that I do listen to you and I am a doer of your word, and I do live in safety, therefore, I am far from fear and oppression.

2 TIMOTHY 1:7

WEEK TWENTY-TWO

Fear thou not; for I am with thee…
Isaiah 41:10

God Is With Me

Be not afraid of sudden fear, neither of the desolation of the wicked, when it cometh.
Proverbs 3:25

Boldly Say: **Father I thank you for you said I should not be afraid of sudden fear, I boldly believe in my heart and confess with mouth that I am not afraid of sudden fear, neither the desolation of the wicked, for you are always with me. It is wonderful to know that God is always with me, what is fear that I should**

fear, no fear here, Jesus is Lord, Jesus is my Lord, the name of Jesus is above fear, and fear is subject to the name of Jesus. Jesus gave me his name to use against all foes.

2 TIMOTHY 1:7

WEEK TWENTY-THREE

Fear thou not; for I am with thee…
Isaiah 41:10

God Is With Me

Say to them that are of a fearful heart, Be strong, fear not: behold, your God will come with vengeance, even God with a recompence; he will come and save you.
Isaiah 35:4

Boldly Say: Father I thank you that vengeance belongs to you. Father I thank you that you will repay. Father I do put on your whole armour, and I do stand against the vice of the evil one, against the evil day, and having done all, I do stand. I am strong and I am strong in the grace of my Lord and Saviour Jesus Christ. I say to myself be strong and of good courage, I am strong and of good courage. I am not afraid, God is with me, and I am not alone.

2 TIMOTHY 1:7

WEEK TWENTY-FOUR

Fear thou not; for I am with thee…
Isaiah 41:10

God Is With Me

Fear thou not; for I am with thee: be not dismayed; for I am thy God: I will strengthen thee; yea, I will help thee; yea, I will uphold thee with the right hand of my righteousness.
Isaiah 41:10

Boldly Say: Father I thank you that I am not afraid because you told me to fear not, that is, I should not be afraid, when my earthly father tells me not to fear, I am never afraid, how much more my heavenly Father tells me not to fear, I refuse to disobey my heavenly Father, I am obedient to my earthly father, I am greatly obedient to my heavenly Father. I have no fear and I am not afraid. God, you said you will help me, I trust you and I believe you will help me in every circumstance.

2 TIMOTHY 1:7

WEEK TWENTY-FIVE

Fear thou not; for I am with thee…
Isaiah 41:10

God Is With Me

For I the LORD thy God will hold thy right hand, saying unto thee, Fear not; I will help thee.
Isaiah 41:13

<u>*Boldly Say:*</u> Father I thank you that you are always with me, I am never alone. Father I thank you for holding my right hand and keeping me from the evil one and you said to me "fear not, I will help thee." Father because you are holding my right hand, and you said to me fear not, you said you will help me,

therefore, I am not afraid. Father I thank you that I do trust you to help me in every situations, circumstances and condition, regardless of its nature.

2 TIMOTHY 1:7

WEEK TWENTY-SIX

Fear thou not; for I am with thee…
Isaiah 41:10

God Is With Me

But now thus saith the L<small>ORD</small> that created thee, O Jacob, and he that formed thee, O Israel, Fear not: for I have redeemed thee, I have called thee by thy name; thou art mine.
Isaiah 43:1

Boldly Say: Father I thank you that you created me in your own image and likeness and you formed me and you do call me by my name. You said to me not to fear, yes my child fear not, I have redeemed you. Father I

thank you that you redeemed me from the devil and from fear. I am not afraid, I belong to God Almighty.

2 TIMOTHY 1:7

WEEK TWENTY-SEVEN

Fear thou not; for I am with thee…
Isaiah 41:10

God Is With Me

Fear not: for I am with thee: I will bring thy seed from the east, and gather thee from the west;
Isaiah 43:5

Boldly Say: **Father I thank you that I am not afraid because you commanded me not to fear. I thank you that you will bring to my possession all that pertaining to me. My children are bless of the Lord, they are far from oppression, they are far from fear, they are established in righteousness, they are not afraid,** they are blessed coming in and going out, they are anointed of the Lord. The anointing of God does abide in them forever.

2 TIMOTHY 1:7

WEEK TWENTY-EIGHT

Fear thou not; for I am with thee…
Isaiah 41:10

God Is With Me

Thus saith the LORD that made thee, and formed thee from the womb, which will help thee; Fear not, O Jacob, my servant; and thou, Jesurun, whom I have chosen.
Isaiah 44:2

Boldly Say: Father I thank you that you made me and formed me from the womb and you said you will help me, I do believe you will do what you said you will do, and therefore, I do rest in you and in your word that lives forever. I thank you that you will help me in every situation. Father, I thank you that I am forever yours; I do forever belongs to you. Father, I thank you that I am bone of the bone of Jesus Christ, and flesh of the flesh of Jesus Christ. Father, I thank you that I am a member of your family forever because I have accepted the sacrificed blood of Jesus Christ. Father, I thank you that there is no fear in me. I have no fear.

2 TIMOTHY 1:7

WEEK TWENTY-NINE

Fear thou not; for I am with thee...
Isaiah 41:10

God Is With Me

Fear ye not, neither be afraid: have not I told thee from that time, and have declared it? ye are even my witnesses. Is there a God beside me? yea, there is no God; I know not any.
Isaiah 44:8

<u>*Boldly Say:*</u> **Father I thank you that you are the Great God; you are the Creator of Heaven and Earth, and all therein. I thank you that there is no God beside thee. All other gods are made by human beings. Therefore, I am**

not afraid. In the world there are several gods, some have eyes that cannot see, legs that cannot move and hands that cannot move: all are made by people. I do serve the True and Living God; therefore, I am not afraid.

2 TIMOTHY 1:7

WEEK THIRTY

Fear thou not; for I am with thee…
Isaiah 41:10

God Is With Me

Hearken unto me, ye that know righteousness, the people in whose heart is my law; fear ye not the reproach of men, neither be ye afraid of their revilings.
Isaiah 51:11

<u>Boldly Say:</u> Father I thank you that Jesus Christ who knew no sin was made sin for me that I might be made your righteousness in Christ Jesus. Father I thank you that you made Jesus Christ righteousness for me. I thank you that Jesus Christ is

my righteousness. Father I thank you that your word is in my heart. Father I thank you for telling me not to fear, Father I thank you that I do obey you, and I am not afraid of men born of women.

2 TIMOTHY 1:7

WEEK THIRTY-ONE

Fear thou not; for I am with thee…
Isaiah 41:10

God Is With Me

In righteousness shalt thou be established: thou shalt be far from oppression; for thou shalt not fear: and from terror; for it shall not come near thee.
Isaiah 54:14

Boldly Say: Father I thank you that I am established in righteousness, Father I thank you that I am far from oppression, Father I thank you that I am not afraid because you tell me not to be afraid, Father I thank you that I am far from terror, for terror shall not come near me. Father I thank you that you have engraved me in the palms of your hands.

2 TIMOTHY 1:7

WEEK THIRTY-TWO

Fear thou not; for I am with thee…
Isaiah 41:10

God Is With Me

But while he thought on these things, behold, the angel of the LORD appeared unto him in a dream, saying, Joseph, thou son of David, fear not to take unto thee Mary thy wife: for that which is conceived in her is of the Holy Ghost.
St. Matthew 1:20

Boldly Say: Father I thank you for your grace that richly abide in me thereby do enable me to obey you when it is even contrary to tradition and culture. I boldly believe in my heart and I boldly confess with my mouth that I am God's obedient child. I am not afraid to obey God in the midst of a crooked and pervert generation. I do speak the truth in love, I love God, I love me and I love people, I boldly confess, I do not leave in fear.

2 TIMOTHY 1:7

WEEK THIRTY-THREE

Fear thou not; for I am with thee...
Isaiah 41:10

God Is With Me

And the angel said unto them, Fear not: for, behold, I bring you good tidings of great joy, which shall be to all people.
St. Luke 2:10

Boldly Say: Father I thank you for your word. Father I thank you that your word is good news, your word gives life, I am not afraid of good news. Religion and tradition of men gives bad news but your word proclaim your goodness, yes! Your word proclaims your unconditional love to me daily. I am not afraid of your daily love for me and towards me.

2 TIMOTHY 1:7

WEEK THIRTY-FOUR

Fear thou not; for I am with thee...
Isaiah 41:10

God Is With Me

But when Jesus heard it, he answered him, saying, Fear not: believe only, and she shall be made whole.

St. Luke 8:50

<u>*Boldly Say:*</u> **Father I thank you that you will not tell me to do what you have not enable me and grace me to do. I am not afraid, because God told me not to fear. I am not afraid to obey God. I am not afraid to act on God's word. God told me not to fear but to believe his word. I**

am a believer of God's word, I am not afraid.

2 TIMOTHY 1:7

WEEK THIRTY-FIVE

Fear thou not; for I am with thee…
Isaiah 41:10

God Is With Me

But even the very hairs of your head are all numbered. Fear not therefore: ye are of more value than many sparrows.
St. Luke 12:7

Boldly Say: Father I thank you that you do take care of everything you created. Father I thank you that I am the crown of your creation. Father, you are my very own Father and I am your very own child, you do take care of the sparrows, how much more me. Father I thank you that I will not doubt you to take care of me. I have no fear, my God is taking care of me. My God is my source, he does supply all my needs and all my needs are met.

2 TIMOTHY 1:7

WEEK THIRTY-SIX

Fear thou not; for I am with thee...
Isaiah 41:10

God Is With Me

Saying, Fear not, Paul; thou must be brought before Caesar: and, lo, God hath given thee all them that sail with thee.
Acts 27:24

Boldly Say: Father I thank you that it shall be to me according to your word. I will obey you and go to wherever you send me and say whatever you tell me to say, for I am not afraid because you told me not to fear and you are with me evermore. Father I thank you that no man shall be able stand before me all the days of my life, as you were with Moses, Joshua, and Jesus Christ, so are you with me. For you will never leave me nor forsake me. Father, you are with me always.

2 TIMOTHY 1:7

WEEK THIRTY-SEVEN

Fear thou not; for I am with thee…
Isaiah 41:10

God Is With Me

For ye have not received the spirit of bondage again to fear; but ye have received the Spirit of adoption, whereby we cry, Abba, Father.
Roman 8:15

Boldly Say: Father I thank you that you have set me free through Jesus Christ, who the Son set free, is free in deed. Jesus Christ has set me free; I refuse to be in bondage again to anything. I thank you Father that I have not received the spirit of bondage again to fear, but I have received from you the Spirit of adoption, whereby I call you Abba Father. Yes, you are my very own Father and I am your very own child. Therefore, I am not afraid.

2 TIMOTHY 1:7

WEEK THIRTY-EIGHT

Fear thou not; for I am with thee…
Isaiah 41:10

God Is With Me

For God hath not given us the spirit of fear; but of power, and of love, and of a sound mind.
2 Timothy 1:7

Boldly Say: Father I thank you that you are my Father, I believe you only give me good stuff, regardless of what religion and the tradition of men may teach about you. Let all men be liar, but God Almighty remains faithful. What Jesus Christ my Lord paid for, I refuse to pay for it again. Father I thank you that

Jesus Christ paid for my redemption once and for all. Yes, Jesus paid for my sins; past, present and future, sickness and diseases, financial lack, peace of mind, and everything the devil took from me due to the fall of Adam and Eve. My salvation is in whole and full, not in part. God did not give me the spirit of fear, therefore, I do not have the spirit of fear, and I boldly confess I have no fear. I have the spirit of power, and of love and of a sound mind.

2 TIMOTHY 1:7

WEEK THIRTY-NINE

Fear thou not; for I am with thee...
Isaiah 41:10

God Is With Me

So that we may boldly say, The Lord is my helper, and I will not fear what man shall do unto me. Hebrews 13:6

Boldly Say: Father I thank you that you are my God and my Father. Father you are my helper, you are my very present helper in time of trouble. Father I trust you, yes I trust you above my feelings. Yes, Father I trust you above my past circumstances, above my present circumstances, and above my future circumstances. Father I trust you helping me above any fear of man's action. What can man do unto me? For God is on my side and God is with me forever regardless of how I feel, God is always with me. I am not afraid of any man.

2 TIMOTHY 1:7

WEEK FORTY

Fear thou not; for I am with thee…
Isaiah 41:10

God Is With Me

There is no fear in love; but perfect love casteth out fear: because fear hath torment. He that feareth is not made perfect in love.
1 John 4:18

Boldly Say: Father I thank you that you are Love and you are my very own Father. I thank you that I am born by Love, I am born of Love, I proceeded from Love, Father I thank you that what is true of you is true of me, for everything begat his or its kind. Therefore, I am love. I have no fear in me because I am love. Father I thank you that there is no fear in love. Father I thank you that perfect love casteth away fear. Father I thank you that I do walk in love, in Jesus name, Amen.

2 TIMOTHY 1:7

WEEK FORTY-ONE

Fear thou not; for I am with thee…
Isaiah 41:10

God Is With Me

Peace I leave with you, my peace I give unto you: not as the world giveth, give I unto you. Let not your heart be troubled, neither let it be afraid.
St. John 14:27

<u>Boldly Say:</u> Father I thank you for the peace which passes all understanding that Jesus Christ gave to me. I will not let my heart be trouble, neither am I afraid about the state of affair of the present world, for I do take Jesus Christ at his word. I am not alone, God is always with me. God is greater than any and all situation that comes my way.

2 TIMOTHY 1:7

WEEK FORTY-TWO

Fear thou not; for I am with thee…
Isaiah 41:10

God Is With Me

Then spake the Lord to Paul in the night by a vision, Be not afraid, but speak, and hold not thy peace:
Acts 18:9

<u>*Boldly Say:*</u> **Father I thank you that you do still speak by vision. Father I thank you that vision has not pass away according to some religious teachings. Father I thank you that you do speak to me any way you choose. Father I thank you that you always tell me not to fear and not to be**

afraid, when the evil one brings fear; you always assure me of your present with me.

2 TIMOTHY 1:7

WEEK FORTY-THREE

Fear thou not; for I am with thee…
Isaiah 41:10

God Is With Me

But and if ye suffer for righteousness' sake, happy are ye: and be not afraid of their terror, neither be troubled;
1 Peter 3:14

Boldly Say: Father I thank you that when people misunderstand the intent of my action, and speak all manner of evil about me and my God way of living, Father I pray your grace will manifest in me to pray for them, and that I will never be afraid of them or their faces. I pray that they will see my continueous bold living for you.

2 TIMOTHY 1:7

WEEK FORTY-FOUR

Fear thou not; for I am with thee…
Isaiah 41:10

God Is With Me

As soon as Jesus heard the word that was spoken, he saith unto the ruler of the synagogue, Be not afraid, only believe.
St. Mark 5:36

Boldly Say: **Father I thank you for your precious word. Father I thank you for teaching me in your word and by your Spirit that dwells in me forever that fear comes from the words spoken by the evil one. But, faith in you comes from your written word and your spoken word.**

Father I thank you that you do not contradict your written word. Father I thank you that I am not afraid; I am a believer in you and in your word. I do believe what you said in your written word about you, about me, and about people.

2 TIMOTHY 1:7

WEEK FORTY-FIVE

**Fear thou not; for I am with thee…
Isaiah 41:10**

God Is With Me

That he would grant unto us, that we being delivered out of the hand of our enemies might serve him without fear,
St. Luke 1:74

Boldly Say: Father I thank you that you have delivered me from the hands of my enemies, and that I should serve you without fear. Father I thank you that I do serve you without fear. I careless what anyone think about my total devotion to you. Father I thank you that I am not ashamed of the gospel of my Lord Jesus Christ, for it is your power unto salvation, yes! Born again, deliverance, divine health, healing, prosperity, baptism of the Holy Ghost and fire, right living and God's supernatural. I am not afraid to receive and enjoy all that was paid by Jesus Christ for me.

2 TIMOTHY 1:7

WEEK FORTY-SIX

**Fear thou not; for I am with thee…
Isaiah 41:10**

God Is With Me

And deliver them who through fear of death were all their lifetime subject to bondage.
Hebrews 2:15

Boldly Say: **Father I thank you that Jesus Christ has delivered me from fear, yes, from fear of death, I have pass from death to life because I have accepted Jesus Christ into my heart and I do love the brethren. He is my Saviour and Lord. Death has no power over me, because to be absent from the body is to be** present with the Lord. As it is written "O death, where is thy sting? O grave, where is thy victory?" also "But thanks be to God, which giveth us the victory through our Lord Jesus Christ." I am forever free from fear.

2 TIMOTHY 1:7

WEEK FORTY-SEVEN

Fear thou not; for I am with thee…
Isaiah 41:10

God Is With Me

Now if Timotheus come, see that he may be with you without fear: for he worketh the work of the Lord, as I also do.
1 Corinthians 16:10

Boldly Say: Father I thank you that I am what I am by your grace. I thank you that fellow Christians are free to fellowship with me regardless of their denomination. I do receive the believers as Jesus Christ received me. I am not afraid to fellowship with fellow believers, as it is written "A new commandment I give unto you, That ye love one another; as I have loved you, that ye also love one another." also "By this shall all men know that ye are my disciples, if ye have love one to another." I am not afraid of religious rules and traditions of men. I do put the word of God above religious rules and traditions of men. Father, I love you, I love me and I do love the believers in Christ Jesus.

2 TIMOTHY 1:7

WEEK FORTY-EIGHT

Fear thou not; for I am with thee…
Isaiah 41:10

God Is With Me

And many of the brethren in the Lord, waxing confident by my bonds, are much more bold to speak the word without fear.
Philippians 1:14

Boldly Say: Father I thank you that you commanded me to share the gospel of Jesus Christ with others, Father I thank you for baptize me with the Holy Ghost and fire. Father I thank you for anointing me with your Holy Spirit, Father I thank you that your Holy Spirit does abide in me forever. Therefore, I am not afraid to share the gospel with others. I do share the gospel with others. I do look for an opportunity or create an opportunity to share the gospel with others.

2 TIMOTHY 1:7

WEEK FORTY-NINE

Fear thou not; for I am with thee…
Isaiah 41:10

God Is With Me

But when he saw the wind boisterous, he was afraid; and beginning to sink, he cried, saying, Lord, save me.

St. Matthew 14:30

Boldly Say: **Father I thank you for your precious word. Father I thank you that when I am confronted with fear, I will not act nice and dignify, I will call on you, yes, I will call on the name of Jesus, which is above every other name. I will speak your victorious word against fear. I** will not analyze the fear, or give thought to what anyone may think, or care what anyone may be thinking, I will boldly declare your word against that fear. I boldly declare to the spirit of fear: I am not afraid of fear and all that comes with it.

2 TIMOTHY 1:7

WEEK FIFTY

Fear thou not; for I am with thee…
Isaiah 41:10

God Is With Me

And I was afraid, and went and hid thy talent in the earth: lo, there thou hast that is thine.
St. Matthew 25:25

<u>*Boldly Say:*</u> Father I thank you for your word. It is written "For the gifts and calling of God are without repentance." Father I thank you for your gifts and calling in my life. I thank you for the boldness you have given me to use your gifts that are in me for your glory and to bless humanity. Father I boldly con-

fess that I do not possess the spirit of fear or intimidation but I do possess the spirit of power, and of love, and of a sound mind.

2 TIMOTHY 1:7

WEEK FIFTY-ONE

Fear thou not; for I am with thee…
Isaiah 41:10

God Is With Me

And I say unto you my friends, Be not afraid of them that kill the body, and after that have no more that they can do.
St. Luke 4:12

Boldly Say: Father I thank you for your word. Your word said the fear of man bring snare. Father I thank you that you have delivered me from people and what people think about me and my love for you. I am move by your love. Father I thank you for a none compromise life. You said to me again and again in your word: fear not, be not afraid. You said also to me greater is he that is in me, than he that is in the world. You said to me: you have not given me the spirit of fear, but of power, and of love and of a sound mind.

2 TIMOTHY 1:7

WEEK FIFTY-TWO

Fear thou not; for I am with thee...
Isaiah 41:10

God Is With Me

Fear not, little flock; for it is your Father's good pleasure to give you the kingdom.
St. Luke 12:32

Boldly Say: Father I thank you that it is your good pleasure to give me the kingdom. Religion and the traditions of men that make your word of no effect taught me to be afraid of you but you continue to teach me daily in your word to reverence you and to love you, for you love me dearly, and you call me daily to come and fellowship with you. In fact you told me to come boldly to you because you love me. You are my very own Father and I am your very own child. The Kingdom is in me now and you rule in me, you do rule in all pertaining to me and your first choice of ruling on earth is through me. I have no fear; I have no worry, for my God does take care of me.

2 TIMOTHY 1:7

SOIL Foundation, Inc.

Publication Books

All Books can be Purchase from amazon.com, Amazon.co.uk, Amazon.de, Amazon.fr, Amazon.it, Amazon.es, Barnesandnoble.com, ebay.com, createspace.com (search: Ovbije Book)

All Day God

Praying the Word From the Book of Timothy

Praying the Word From the Book of Ephesians

Resurrection from the Flood

Coaching to Completion

Praying the Word From the Epistle of John

God Loves Me

God Is With Me I Am Not Afraid

Libros en Español

**Orando la Palabra
Desde el Libro de Efesios**

Dios Me Ama

Tracts:

5 Things God wants you to know

Love Yourself

www.ingramcontent.com/pod-product-compliance
Lightning Source LLC
Chambersburg PA
CBHW070522030426
42337CB00016B/2066